Nn

Bela Davis

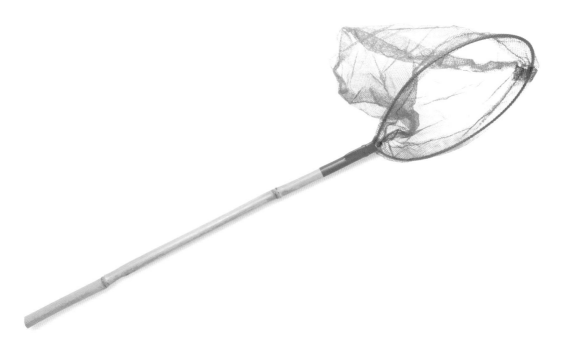

Abdo
THE ALPHABET
Kids

abdopublishing.com

Published by Abdo Kids, a division of ABDO, PO Box 398166, Minneapolis, Minnesota 55439.
Copyright © 2017 by Abdo Consulting Group, Inc. International copyrights reserved in all countries.
No part of this book may be reproduced in any form without written permission from the publisher.

Printed in the United States of America, North Mankato, Minnesota.

102016
012017

THIS BOOK CONTAINS
RECYCLED MATERIALS

Photo Credits: iStock, Shutterstock, Thinkstock

Production Contributors: Teddy Borth, Jennie Forsberg, Grace Hansen

Design Contributors: Christina Doffing, Candice Keimig, Dorothy Toth

Publisher's Cataloging in Publication Data

Names: Davis, Bela, author.

Title: Nn / by Bela Davis.

Description: Minneapolis, Minnesota : Abdo Kids, 2017 | Series: The alphabet |
    Includes bibliographical references and index.

Identifiers: LCCN 2016943895 | ISBN 9781680808902 (lib. bdg.) |
    ISBN 9781680796001 (ebook) | ISBN 9781680796674 (Read-to-me ebook)

Subjects: LCSH: English language--Alphabet--Juvenile literature. | Alphabet
    books--Juvenile literature.

Classification: DDC 421/.1--dc23

LC record available at http://lccn.loc.gov/2016943895

Table of Contents

Nn 4

More Nn Words . . . 22

Glossary 23

Index 24

Abdo Kids Code . . . 24

Nn

Nora makes a lot of **n**oise.

Nn

Nala **n**eeds to lear**n** her **lines**.

Nn

Nola**n** stands **n**ear **N**ia.

Nn

Naomi **tends** to **N**ick's k**n**ee.

Nn

Nina scored **n**ine points.

13

Nn

Nate thinks the **n**est is **n**eat!

Nn

Noah has a **n**ew **n**eighbor.

Nn

Nadia is **n**ice to her frie**n**ds.

19

Nn

What does **N**atalie touch?

(her **n**ose)

More **Nn** Words

neck

nickel

newspaper

nurse

Glossary

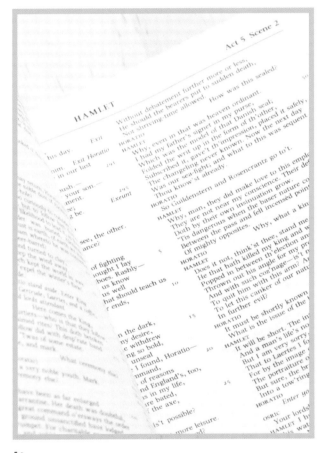

lines
the words of a part in a play.

neighbor
a person who lives next to or near another person.

tend
to apply oneself to the care of.

Index

friend 18

knee 10

learn 6

lines 6

near 8

neighbor 16

nest 14

nice 18

noise 4

nose 20

score 12

abdokids.com

Use this code to log on to abdokids.com and access crafts, games, videos, and more!

Abdo Kids Code:
TNK8902